Dear Parent:

Congratulations! Your child is taking the first steps on an exciting journey. The destination? Independent reading!

STEP INTO READING® will help your child get there. The program offers five steps to reading success. Each step includes fun stories and colorful art. There are also Step into Reading Sticker Books, Step into Reading Math Readers, Step into Reading Write-In Readers, Step into Reading Phonics Readers, and Step into Reading Phonics First Steps! Boxed Sets—a complete literacy program with something for every child.

Learning to Read, Step by Step!

Ready to Read   Preschool–Kindergarten
• big type and easy words • rhyme and rhythm • picture clues
For children who know the alphabet and are eager to begin reading.

Reading with Help   Preschool–Grade 1
• basic vocabulary • short sentences • simple stories
For children who recognize familiar words and sound out new words with help.

Reading on Your Own   Grades 1–3
• engaging characters • easy-to-follow plots • popular topics
For children who are ready to read on their own.

Reading Paragraphs   Grades 2–3
• challenging vocabulary • short paragraphs • exciting stories
For newly independent readers who read simple sentences with confidence.

Ready for Chapters   Grades 2–4
• chapters • longer paragraphs • full-color art
For children who want to take the plunge into chapter books but still like colorful pictures.

STEP INTO READING® is designed to give every child a successful reading experience. The grade levels are only guides. Children can progress through the steps at their own speed, developing confidence in their reading, no matter what their grade.

Remember, a lifetime love of reading starts with a single step!

*For the two coolest Yankee fans I know: my
brother-in-law and friend John Gisondi and
my colleague and friend Jim Kinkead
—F.M.*

*For Viria, so passionate about her Yankees
—R.W.*

Author acknowledgments: Thank you to Shana Corey's magical eye as an editor. Thanks to
Freddy Berowski, library associate at the National Baseball Hall of Fame and Museum, for
his assistance and expertise. *Babe: The Legend Comes to Life* by Robert W. Creamer, *The
Yankees* by Phil Pepe, *A Yankee Century* by Harvey Frommer, and *Babe Ruth and the 1918
Red Sox* by Allan Wood served as the best resources, among others.

Photo credit: Photo courtesy of the Hall family.

www.stepintoreading.com

Educators and librarians, for a variety of teaching tools, visit us at
www.randomhouse.com/teachers

Library of Congress Cataloging-in-Publication Data
Murphy, Frank.
Babe Ruth saves baseball! / by Frank Murphy ; illustrated by Richard Walz. — 1st ed.
   p. cm. — (Step into reading)
ISBN 0-375-83048-0 (trade) — ISBN 0-375-93048-5 (lib. bdg.)
1. Ruth, Babe, 1895–1948—Juvenile literature. 2. Baseball players—United States—
Biography—Juvenile literature. [1. Ruth, Babe, 1895–1948. 2. Baseball players.
3. Baseball—History.] I. Walz, Richard, ill. II. Title. III. Series.
GV865.R8M87 2005   796.357'092—dc22   2003027464

Printed in the United States of America
First Edition   10 9 8 7

STEP INTO READING® STEP 3

BABE RUTH
Saves Baseball!

by Frank Murphy
illustrated by Richard Walz

Random House 🏠 New York

Almost everyone knows

something about

George Herman Ruth.

You probably know him as Babe—

that was his nickname.

Babe played for the

New York Yankees.

He hit hundreds of home runs.

Most people think he

was baseball's greatest player.

But do you know the *best* thing

about Babe Ruth?

He saved baseball.

He did!

Here's how it happened.

The story starts off in 1914—

Babe Ruth's first year

in the major leagues.

Baseball was America's

favorite sport.

Fans read about games

in newspapers.

Kids collected cards
of their favorite players.

And people filled ballparks

to cheer on their favorite teams.

Baseball was Babe's
favorite sport, too.
Believe it or not,
Babe wasn't always a Yankee.
Babe played for
the Boston Red Sox.

In those days,

Babe was a pitcher—not a hitter.

Babe threw fast.

Babe threw strikes.

And he almost always won.

Pitchers don't play every day.

So pitchers don't hit that often.

But Babe practiced hitting.

He loved to swing the bat.

He loved to hit the ball.

And boy, could Babe hit!

In 1915, Babe hit
his first home run.
It was against
the New York Yankees!
He hit it hard.
He hit it high.
And he hit it far.

Fans cheered.
They had never seen
a home run quite like it.

People began to wonder,

why isn't Babe a hitter?

"Babe, get ready to bat more!"

said Babe's coach.

Babe still had to pitch

in some games.

But now he got to play every day!

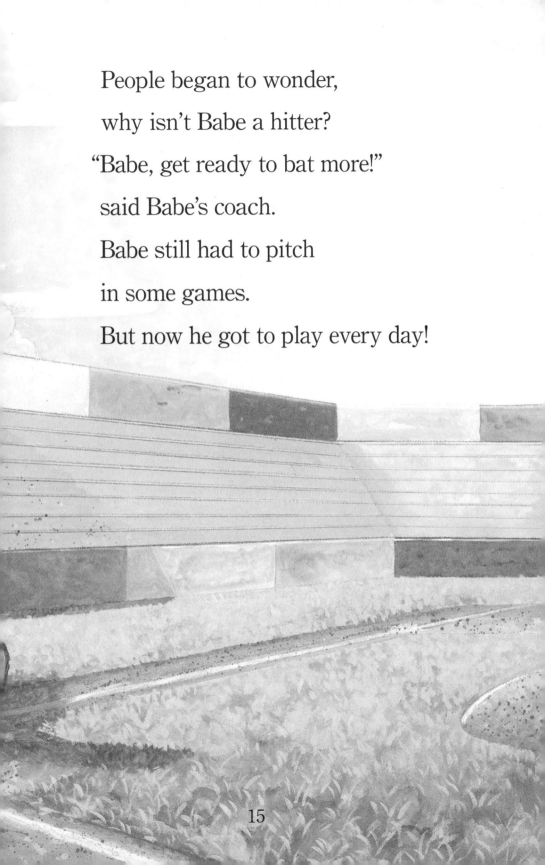

In 1919, Babe hit the most
home runs ever—29.
In every city he played in,
people kept track of
Babe's home runs.

Babe kept track, too—

by carving notches in his bat!

And Babe hit at least one

home run in every city he visited.

No one had done that before.

Babe became

the king of home runs!

In that year, something bad
happened to baseball.
Fans were excited
about the World Series.
They wanted to find out
which team was the best—
the Chicago White Sox
or the Cincinnati Reds.

But some White Sox
players cheated.
People all across America
found out.

People were shocked.

Many fans stopped

going to the ball fields.

A boy saw his favorite

White Sox player.

"Say it ain't so, Joe!"

the boy cried.

But it *was* so.

People just didn't trust
baseball anymore.

Baseball needed someone who
could make fans care again.

But who was big enough
to save baseball?

Babe Ruth—that's who!

In 1920, something good
happened to Babe Ruth.
Babe went to play for a new team,
the New York Yankees.
Babe knew that meant
no more pitching—just hitting.
Babe met his new teammates
in New York City.
"I'm Babe Ruth.
Let's play ball!" he said.

People wondered,
could Babe hit
29 home runs again?
"I'll hit 50 this year," he promised.
"Impossible!" people said.

The season started.

Game after game,

Babe clubbed home runs.

The more Babe hit,

the more people paid attention.

"That Babe Ruth sure can hit!"

they said.

Newspaper boys

shouted out the news.

"Babe hits another! Yankees win!"

And Babe was right!

He hit a lot more than

29 that year—he hit 54!

"Wow! Babe Ruth really

keeps his word!" people said.

Babe was changing
people's minds about baseball.
And Babe's home runs
changed baseball.
Now every team tried
to hit more home runs.
Other players even tried
to copy Babe's swing.
That meant more runs
and more excitement!

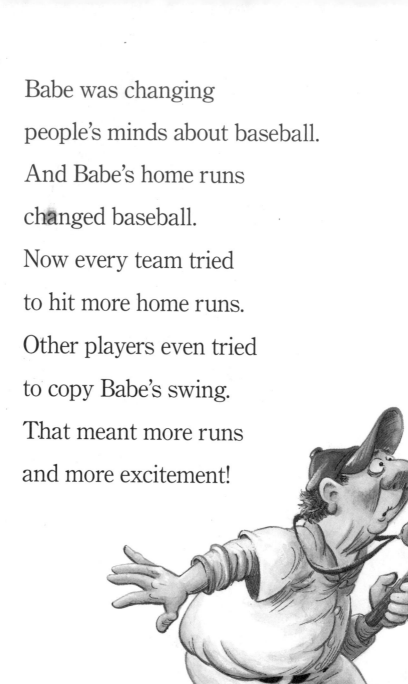

Babe loved children.

So he did something fun for them.

He signed hundreds of baseballs.

Then he hid them.

Children raced around town

to find them!

More and more fans
came to watch Babe!
People were too crowded.

The Yankees needed more seats.

So they built a new ballpark.

And it was big—

just like Babe's home runs.

"Some ball yard!" Babe said.

For the first time
people called a ballpark
something different—a stadium.
It was named Yankee Stadium.
But one reporter had a better idea.
He remembered why they built it.
So he nicknamed it
"The House That Ruth Built."

On April 18, 1923,

the gates opened.

A marching band played music.

The American flag was raised.

Babe's old team,

the Boston Red Sox,

came to play!

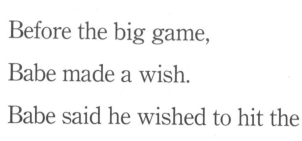

Before the big game,

Babe made a wish.

Babe said he wished to hit the

first home run in Yankee Stadium.

Everyone waited to see

if Babe could do it.

The governor of New York

threw out the first ball.

The umpire shouted,

"Play ball!"

By the fourth inning,
the Yankees were winning.
But no one had hit
a home run yet.
Babe came up to bat.
Fans held their breath.

People listened to their radios.

Everyone wanted to know

if Babe's wish would come true.

The pitcher threw the ball.

Babe swung with all his might.

Whack!

The radio announcer called out,

"He did it! He did it!

Babe Ruth hits the first home run

ever at Yankee Stadium!"

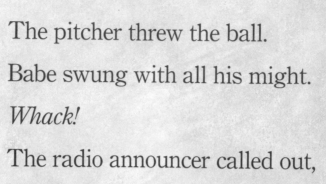

Babe jogged around the bases.

The crowd stood and cheered.

"Hooray for Babe!"

"Hooray for baseball!"

Babe crossed home plate.

He lifted his cap and

waved to the fans.

Then he bowed.

His wish had come true.

Babe hit a total of 714 home runs
in his career.
He was one of the first
players elected to the
National Baseball Hall of Fame.
Today people remember Babe as
the greatest baseball player ever.

Almost everyone knows
something about Babe Ruth.
But now you know the best thing
about Babe Ruth—
how he saved baseball.

AUTHOR'S NOTE

Babe Ruth really did care
about saving baseball.
He said, "I won't be happy until
we have every boy in America . . .
between the ages of six and sixteen
wearing a glove and swinging a bat."
Today millions of boys *and girls* play
baseball—in part because of Babe!

Babe Ruth signs an autograph for eight-year-old Gordon Hall.